My Own

Mass

Booklet

Name Eduardo

My first celebration of
the Sacrament of the Eucharist:

Date May 3, 2014

Parish St Patrick

City Carlsbad

State C A

I Celebrate the Lord's Day

I keep the Lord's Day holy. I gather with God's family at Mass. I also rest from work, spend time with my family, and help others.

This is a picture of me celebrating the Lord's Day.

I can go to Mass on Saturday evening or on Sunday.

These are some of the people from my parish whom I see at Mass.

Write the names of people you see at church.

_____

_____

_____

_____

We Celebrate Mass

Introductory Rites

We gather in God's presence.

Entrance Chant

The priest, deacon, ministers, and servers process to the altar. We stand and sing a song praising God.

Greeting

The priest greets all who are gathered.

Priest: In the name of the Father, and of the Son, and of the Holy Spirit.

People: Amen.

Priest: The grace of our Lord Jesus Christ, and the love of God, and the communion of the Holy Spirit be with you all.

People: And with your spirit.

Penitential Act

We admit that we have sinned. We ask God for mercy. We pray together.

I confess to almighty God
and to you, my brothers and sisters,
that I have greatly sinned,
in my thoughts and in my words,
in what I have done and in what I have failed
    to do,

Then, we strike our breast and say:

through my fault, through my fault,
through my most grievous fault;
therefore I ask blessed Mary ever-Virgin,
all the Angels and Saints,
and you, my brothers and sisters,
to pray for me to the Lord
    our God.

Lord, have mercy.

Kyrie (Lord Have Mercy)

Priest: Lord, have mercy.

People: Lord, have mercy.

Priest: Christ, have mercy.

People: Christ, have mercy.

Priest: Lord, have mercy.

People: Lord, have mercy.

Priest: May almighty God have mercy
on us,
forgive us our sins,
and bring us to everlasting life.

People: Amen.

Christ, have mercy.

Gloria

We sing praise to God in these words.

Glory to God in the highest,
and on earth peace to people of good will.

We praise you,
we bless you,
we adore you,
we glorify you,
we give you thanks for your great glory,
Lord God, heavenly King,
O God, almighty Father.

Lord Jesus Christ, Only Begotten Son,
Lord God, Lamb of God, Son of the Father,
you take away the sins of the world,
     have mercy on us;
you take away the sins of the world,
     receive our prayer;

Help me color
this page.

you are seated at the right hand of the Father,
   have mercy on us.

For you alone are the Holy One,
you alone are the Lord,
you alone are the Most High,
Jesus Christ,
with the Holy Spirit,
in the glory of God the Father.
Amen.

Collect Prayer

The priest invites us to pray.
We respond:

Help me trace these letters.

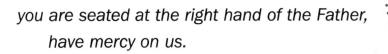

Liturgy of the Word

We sit and listen to God's Word.

First Reading

The lector proclaims the first reading. It's usually from the Old Testament. Sometimes it's from the Acts of the Apostles.

We honor God's Word by our response at the end of the reading.

Lector: The Word of the Lord.

People: Thanks be to God.

Responsorial Psalm

The leader of song sings the verses of the psalm. We all sing the refrain.

Second Reading

The lector reads from one of the books in the New Testament that is not a Gospel.

At the end of this reading, he says:

Lector: The Word of the Lord.

People: Thanks be to God.

Gospel

We stand and sing the Gospel Acclamation, an Alleluia, or other words of praise.

Priest or deacon: The Lord be with you.

People: And with your spirit.

Priest or deacon: A reading from the holy Gospel according to (Matthew, Mark, Luke, or John).

People: Glory to you, O Lord.

We trace a cross on our foreheads, lips, and hearts. We pray that God's Word will be in my mind, on my lips, and in my heart.

The priest or deacon proclaims the Gospel.

Then he prays:

Priest or deacon: The Gospel of the Lord.

We respond:

People: Praise to you, Lord Jesus Christ.

Homily

We listen to the homily. The priest or deacon helps us understand the readings. He tells us how to live what we have heard.

Help me trace the crosses.

Profession of Faith

We stand and pray the Creed.

I believe in one God,
the Father almighty,
maker of heaven and earth,
of all things visible and invisible.

I believe in one Lord Jesus Christ,
the Only Begotten Son of God,
born of the Father before all ages.
God from God, Light from Light,
true God from true God,
begotten, not made, consubstantial with
*   the Father;*
through him all things were made.
For us men and for our salvation
he came down from heaven,
and by the Holy Spirit was incarnate of the
*   Virgin Mary,*
and became man.

For our sake he was crucified under Pontius
    Pilate,
he suffered death and was buried,
and rose again on the third day
in accordance with the Scriptures.
He ascended into heaven
and is seated at the right hand of the Father.
He will come again in glory
to judge the living and the dead
and his kingdom will have no end.

I believe in the Holy Spirit, the Lord, the giver
    of life,
who proceeds from the Father and the Son,
who with the Father and the Son is adored and
    glorified,
who has spoken through the prophets.

I believe in one, holy, catholic and apostolic
    Church.
I confess one Baptism for the forgiveness
    of sins
and I look forward to the resurrection
    of the dead
and the life of the world to come. Amen.

Prayer of the Faithful

We present our needs to God. We pray for the Church, for the world, for people in need, and for ourselves.

After each petition, the leader of prayer may say:

> We pray to the Lord.

We answer with these or similar words:

> Lord, hear our prayer.

I'll pray for _Mom_ _because she has a frozen sholeder._

Liturgy of the Eucharist

We bring our gifts to the altar.
We celebrate Christ's presence in
the Eucharist.

Presentation and Preparation of the Gifts

We sit and sing a hymn. At this time,
the gifts of bread and wine are brought
to the altar. The altar is prepared.

We give money in the collection. The
money supports the work of the Church.
It helps people in need. We also give the
time and help we've offered to others.

We ask God to accept and bless our gifts.
The priest holds up the bread and prays.

Priest: Blessed are you, Lord God of
all creation,
for through your goodness
we have received
the bread we offer you:
fruit of the earth and work of
human hands,
it will become for us the
bread of life.

People: Blessed be God for ever.

Then he raises the wine and prays.

Priest: Blessed are you, Lord God of
all creation,
for through your goodness
we have received
the wine we offer you:
fruit of the vine and work of
human hands,
it will become our spiritual drink.

People: Blessed be God for ever.

We stand as the priest prays over the gifts. He asks that God will accept our sacrifice.

Priest: Pray, brothers and sisters, that my sacrifice and yours may be acceptable to God, the almighty Father.

People: May the Lord accept the sacrifice at your hands for the praise and glory of his name, for our good and the good of all his holy Church.

Eucharistic Prayer

God gives us everything that is good. We thank and praise him in the **Preface.**

Priest: The Lord be with you.

People: And with your spirit.

Priest: Lift up your hearts.

People: We lift them up to the Lord.

Priest: Let us give thanks to the Lord our God.

People: It is right and just.

Draw some of God's gifts here.

The priest continues praying words of thanks and praise.

Then all sing or pray the **Holy, Holy, Holy.**

Holy, Holy, Holy Lord God of hosts.
Heaven and earth are full of your glory.
Hosanna in the highest.
Blessed is he who comes in the name of the Lord.
Hosanna in the highest.

We kneel and continue praying the Eucharistic Prayer. We remember Jesus' Last Supper. We remember his sacrifice on the cross. We do as Jesus taught.

The **Consecration** begins. The bread and wine become the Body and Blood of Jesus Christ. Through the power of the Holy Spirit and the words and actions of the priest, Christ is present with us.

I made this chalice beautiful.

We recall all Jesus has done to save us.
We proclaim the **Mystery of Faith.**

Priest: The mystery of faith:

People: We proclaim your Death,
  O Lord,
and profess your Resurrection
until you come again.

The Eucharistic Prayer ends with the
Concluding Doxology and an **Amen.**

Priest: Through him, and with him,
    and in him,
    O God, almighty Father,
    in the unity of the Holy Spirit,
    all glory and honor is yours,
    for ever and ever.

People:  Amen.

Help me color
the letters.

Communion Rite

We stand as we prepare to receive the Body and Blood of Christ in Holy Communion.

Lord's Prayer
Together we pray:

Our Father, who art in heaven,
hallowed be thy name;
thy kingdom come,
thy will be done
on earth as it is in heaven.
Give us this day our daily bread,
and forgive us our trespasses,
as we forgive those who trespass against us;
and lead us not into temptation,
but deliver us from evil.

Priest: Deliver us, Lord, we pray, from
  every evil,
graciously grant peace in our days,
that, by the help of your mercy,
we may be always free from sin
and safe from all distress,
as we await the blessed hope
and the coming of our Savior,
  Jesus Christ.

Together we pray the **Doxology:**

People: For the kingdom,
the power and the glory are yours now
and for ever.

Sign of Peace

The priest prays that we will be united with one another in Christ's peace.

Priest: The peace of the Lord be with you always.

People: And with your spirit.

Then the priest or deacon invites us to offer a sign of peace to those around us.

We exchange a greeting of peace.

Draw yourself exchanging the greeting of peace.

The priest breaks the consecrated host.

Lamb of God

At this time, we all sing or pray aloud:

*Lamb of God, you take away the sins of
the world,*
  have mercy on us.
*Lamb of God, you take away the sins of
the world,*
  have mercy on us.
*Lamb of God, you take away the sins of
the world,*
  grant us peace.

Communion

We kneel as we prepare to receive Holy Communion. The priest raises the host and the chalice. We pray.

Priest: Behold the Lamb of God,
behold him who takes away the sins of the world.
Blessed are those called to the supper of the Lamb.

People: Lord, I am not worthy
that you should enter under my roof,
but only say the word
and my soul shall be healed.

The priest receives Holy Communion. Then he offers the Body and Blood of Christ to the deacon and the extraordinary ministers of Holy Communion.

We receive Holy Communion from a priest, a deacon, or an extraordinary minister of Holy Communion.

We bow in reverence. We receive the Body of Christ—under the form of bread—in our hands or on our tongue.

Priest: The Body of Christ.

People: Amen.

We bow in reverence. We receive the Blood of Christ under the form of wine.

Priest: The Blood of Christ.

People: Amen.

We return to our places and pray quietly. We thank Jesus for the gift of himself in the Eucharist.

We take some time to pray silently.

Prayer after Communion

The priest invites us to stand. He leads us in prayer. He asks God to help us live as followers of Jesus. We answer:

AMEN.

Concluding Rites

Final Blessing

We continue standing as the priest blesses us.

Priest: The Lord be with you.

People: And with your spirit.

Priest: May almighty God bless you, the Father, and the Son, and the Holy Spirit.

People: Amen.

Dismissal

As Mass ends, we are sent to glorify the Lord by our lives at home, at work, and in the world.

Priest or deacon: Go in peace, glorifying the Lord by your life.

Help me color these pages.

People: Thanks be to God.

We sing a joyful closing hymn. Then we leave church happy to live as followers of Jesus.